Own It! In your 20's:

A Guide to Homeownership for the Millennial

Angelo Mirville

Copyright © 2018 Angelo Mirville

ISBN: 1981378995
ISBN-13: 978-1981378999

Own It In Your 20's:

A Guide to Homeownership for the Millennial

A Climbing Companion LLC Partnership

DEDICATION

Mom you already know, but before the waterworks start let me just get this dedication out of the way. Writing this book and building my enterprise brand have been a challenge but in the same way you have been the perfect example of a true nurturer, so have I also been able to implement the principles of a nurturer into my visions and ideas. My first book I have ever successfully written and published by myself, I dedicate to you Mom! Without you I don't believe any of my success would have been possible. Thank You for pushing me and loving me like only a mother can.

Cheers to you!

CONTENTS

ACKNOWLEDGMENTS

We have to acknowledge a few star players before we get started!

My Parents thank you for being the strong foundation and support system.

My Broker Kito J. Johnson you are the epitome of what a true mentor should be and your impact and influence has stretched far beyond real estate. Thank you for believing in my vision!

My productivity coach David Patterson, sir I am so blessed to have a coach that can tell it like it is and push my expectations of myself to new heights.

Thank You All for Supporting me!

FOREWORD

by: Kito J. Johnson

ii

People always ask me how I managed to start a construction business in my 20s, obtain a college degree, build a lengthy portfolio of investment properties, and become a licensed real estate broker, investor and CEO of one of Atlanta's fastest growing and most unique brokerages--all by my late 30s! They ask what I did to get where I am today, and how *they* can do it, too.

Like a predetermined destiny, creating wealth through real estate is something that has followed me and attached itself to everything I do.

I first stumbled upon real estate investing at 20 years old, when a distressed home fell into my lap. I had the chance to purchase it from someone who was looking to sell fast. I was planning to move out of my parents' home, and a friend of mine knew I was interested in buying my first house. Being so young and having no solid real estate education, mentor, or hand to hold through the process, I had to rely on my own gut and knack for being resourceful. I jumped in head first and learned as I went along. I lived in that house for a couple of years, purchased another one, and later successfully flipped my original purchase. After closing that deal, I decided that this was something I wanted to pursue.

By the age of 30, I had acquired 17 rental properties. However, like many during the economic recession of 2008, I was hit hard. I lost all of them but two. This was less a result of the economic downfall as it was a lack of knowledge on my part *as an investor*. After two decades of being in the business, I now realize that my loss was really due to a lack of proper education. If I had known the strategies I know now, I'd still have all of those properties today and then some.

Having learned early that persistence is the key to overcoming challenges, I kept at it until I rebuilt my credit and eventually surpassed my original portfolio value. I've now decorated my experience with more than 1000 transactions. And by applying the smaller details that the top investors have used, I have made my business *recession-proof.*

With the success I've found, it has become the driving force behind my life's mission to educate as much of the population as possible, teaching them how to create generational wealth through the vehicle of real estate. It is very important to me that I use my platform to uplift and empower others to achieve the level of prosperity that the industry has given to me. It is an opportunity open to anyone with enough determination to pursue it.

As a strong man of faith, I believe God puts people in our lives to further us along our journeys. Angelo came to me pursuing his license to be a real estate agent. He had detailed goals for the future. I immediately recognized his drive and enthusiasm for the industry. I knew he was serious about his vision. He already had a full-time job, but was looking to get into investing. Like me, he had acquired his first home at the age of 20. He was goal-oriented, practical, but most importantly, *coachable.* He had a brain like a sponge that soaked up all of the knowledge I had given him. In a few short months, Angelo became one of my star agents, in addition to building an impressive investment track record in a short amount of time.

As I've coached and trained others in recent years, I've realized I appeal to a younger audience of a certain intellectual caliber, much like Angelo. Many knock the younger generation for being inefficient, lazy, and entitled; but in this industry I tend to meet a lot of young, fired-up, business-minded youth who are hungry to earn their place in the world. Many are open, teachable, and looking for mentors to help them further their aspirations and reach their goals.

It's never too early to be successful. It's never too early to set a goal and put a plan into action. We are living in an age where knowledge is at our fingertips. While our parents had to wait or do things the long way for pretty much everything in life, we don't. Life is faster, growth is faster, knowledge is faster. If we put our minds to something, there is virtually nothing stopping us.

The evolution of real estate has brought about a pioneering movement of marrying together the traditional side with the investment side of the industry. More people are getting educated and jumping on this wave of opportunity. It is a tremendous honor of mine to get to mentor enthusiastic twenty-somethings like Angelo who are thinking on an elevated level, ahead of their peers.

Create a mentality within yourself that embodies this great change we're seeing. Why wait? Who governs the standard for what we should or may achieve at any given age? There are no limits. You too, can Own It! In Your 20's.

Kito j. Johnson
CEO of Buy n Sell Inc.
Founder of The Generational Wealth University
www.kitojjohnson.com

Own It!

Introduction
Flat Tire

Photographed in 2015
Angelo's first home purchase at 20 years old

Introduction
Flat Tire

◆ ───────────

It was Spring 2015, sometime at the beginning of April, although I can't quite remember the exact date, I can recall that it was a beautiful spring day in Atlanta, Georgia. This particular day I had taken an unfamiliar route to my barbershop clear across town from my apartment complex; when it happened. I am quite sure I was blasting my favorite worship song this particular day, in my little Toyota Corolla LE, allowing my positive and uplifting juices to flow, so why this unfortunate event happened to me at that moment is beyond my understanding.

"Oh shit!" I uttered, and yes my worship music still blaring in the background, my little black Corolla starts to jerk and swerve out of control.

A flat tire!

I would consider myself an expert driver if I do say so myself, so I was able to get over to the shoulder safely, but now I had to wait for some help, and now burdened with the cost and time that I was about to waste.

The reason why I'm sharing this short back story is simple; I want to show you how a random, seemingly messed up situation, can be the very reason your life is set up to go on a completely different trajectory than you thought. Well completely different to you and others but no surprise to the universe (but that's an entire sermon for another book). If my tire had not blown that day, then the rest of this book would have probably not happened or the title would be "I'm 30+...I need to buy now". If my tire would not have blown that day, the next millennial in line to be a homeowner would miss out on the motivation and encouragement my insight and experience brings.

Well it happened that day, and the shoulder I ended up on was right at the entrance of a gorgeous neighborhood of new construction homes. Many of which were still being constructed. There were balloons and signs letting prospects know of the price ranges, which I knew I couldn't afford. A sign that read 'agent onsite' had my curiosity on a venture of the possibilities of homeownership, at 20 years young.

Well, I wandered into the subdivision, walked quite a ways, passing beautiful ranch and two story homes, foundations being laid, and finishing touches being executed, when voila! I see it. My curiosity slowly turning into determination, as I approached this ranch brick home, with no grass yet laid, and contractors finishing up on the roof working away. The garage was open and it looked like the front door was open too. "Hey!" I yelled up at the workers on the roof top. "May I?" Pointing at the front door. Once I got my shoulder shrug of approval I helped myself.

"Oop! No grass and no carpet yet", I thought to myself, I clearly had to see beyond what I was seeing. I walked into an open floor plan, and scurried through the 3-bedroom 2-bathroom house like a kid in a candy store. The kitchen was decked with stainless steel; the master bedroom was huge! With an on-suite, and the closet was sickening! In a good way of course, a nice big walk in closet. My heart raced at the possibility of no longer renting an apartment but owning this home. I literally fell in love and I just had to have it, but there was only one issue. Where was I going to find $135,000? Can I even get approved for a loan? Don't I need a down payment? Yep just as quickly as I allowed myself to get excited, I couldn't stop doubting the process.

Lot #74 was the only way to identify the property, there wasn't yet an address or even a mailbox. I was freaking out; all I knew was I needed to get to the agent on-site before she left so I could bombard her with questions!

The model home where the agent was working, was very inviting, I can only imagine what she thought when she saw me walk into her office standing 5'5, looking like the young twenty-year-old I indeed was.

"Hi, I would like to know how much for Lot #74?" I asked as if I had it all cash ready, which was definitely not the case. She asked me to come in and invited me to have a seat.

Trust me, I did not expect to end up the owner of a brand new 3-bedroom 2-bathroom home or even writing a book sharing my home-buying experience, but everything truly happens for a reason. What seemed to be an inconvenient day, of time and money wasted replacing a tire, Turned into a productive and life changing moment.

Now 3 years later, a successful licensed real estate agent and real estate investor in the state of Georgia, I have learned so much through my experience as a buyer and through facilitating my clients in the home buying process.

I hope to share an in depth understanding of homeownership, how to-s, facts, tips, and encouragement. That way by the time you decide you are ready whether 20 or 120, you will be able to move forward with boldness and a clear objective.

Chapter I

Buy vs Rent

buy   rent

Chapter 1
Buy vs Rent

───────────── ◆ ─────────────

This comparison has been the topic of discussion across many social classes and real estate enthusiast. Yes, it is somewhat bias for me to stay neutral on the topic as a licensed agent and homeowner myself, however allow me to just lay down a few facts first, then I'll interject my opinion and advice, and let you do your own soul searching. Unless you're a gypsy we all will have to face the reality of whether to buy or rent. Even those who are fortunate enough to have inherited property, have to face this reality. No matter how property is acquired it has to be managed, paid for in some capacity whether in the form of a property tax bill, rent, or mortgage payment. No one is safe from making a decision on the subject matter. With that thought let's dive right in!

Now Let's be very clear, there is nothing and I do mean absolutely nothing wrong with a renter in this world. I've come in contact with quite a few real estate bullies, that will try to induce you into buying a home. The truth of the matter is, buying if approached the wrong way and without the proper guidance, can create a host of issues for you. That is why I am glad you picked up this book, for some guidance and clarity, to gain a little more insight on the American dream of homeownership, instead of going it alone. My objective is in no way to force any opinion on you but to give you tidbits of wisdom based on experience, for you to take and apply to both your quest for real estate knowledge and your life.

As a renter, you'll find that it can turn out to be an excellent way to get used to handling living expenses, especially fresh out of high school and/or college. The reality is that renting seems to be the easiest avenue apart from staying with mom and dad nowadays. In fact, It seems to be a trend among my generation and age group to stay with our parents for as long as we can. Sometimes I wish I shared that mentality, but then again I wouldn't be writing this book had I settled with staying in my parent's home. Granted my parents weren't playing those reindeer games with me, once I left to college It was out for good. I do understand however that that is not everyone's experience; but whatever your ambitions are, make it your business to make provisions to leave the nest and acquire your own sanctuary, I promise you won't regret it or turn back.

Apartment Rental

The most popular form of renting for the typical twenty-year old, would be the traditional apartment. Depending on the city you reside in, determining the average cost to rent in your area and finding the most reasonable price can sometimes be a daunting task. We all know that you get what you pay for when it comes to most things in life, rentals are not excused from that, not by a long shot. The cheaper the apartment, the less desirable the location, appearance, and several other aspects of the living space will be. The opposite is true of the costlier places to rent such as high rises. You will definitely get those beautiful finishes, endless amenities, and perfect location all for the highest price. This trend is consistent throughout the country and all major cities. Searching for an apartment is not at all impossible, in fact I am sure in the city you are currently in, you have more than likely seen several major new construction projects of massive residential buildings being constructed, and huge "now leasing" signs even way before construction is complete. This tells us that investors are taking advantage of this traditional notion that a generation coming up won't be looking to purchase real estate anytime soon or even have the buying power to do so. Will we prove them wrong?

Requiring a simple application and proof of income, some leasing applications don't even require an extensive credit check, this makes renting pretty easy to get moved in. The process is definitely not like applying for a home loan, lenders literally dig into your life to make sure you will be able to amortize your note, aka pay your mortgage on time. Apartment living turns out to be the most appealing and convenient means for living, especially for those that are able to find units with the nicely renovated and modernized layout, decked out with the granite counter tops, fancy security gates, community pools, and 5-star property management for an affordable price. It's easy to be lured into the renting cycle and get comfortable with the lifestyle, trust me I know, I have had my share of apartment dwellings. The oh-so easy application process in itself would make anyone favor just renting over getting into the housing market. Trying to buy a home is just simply intimidating.

Settling for an apartment would be ideal for most of us to "save" until we are "ready" to buy, but let's just be honest the average American has less than $1000 in their savings, and for the millennial, well don't even make me laugh. If you are one of the few that have a savings started and have been consistent, I commend you. Trust me I know that everyone's story is different, so everyone's life experience will be different, however there is a commonality we all share, and that is the desire for stability and financial freedom, and at the end of the day the only thing in the way of us achieving our goals and desires is ourselves. Once we broaden our mental capacity, then the possibilities of success in our lives is truly endless. We all know how important having a savings account is, and agree that being able to save up for a down-payment is extremely important when buying your first home. Just trust me it is possible, it is not as much as you think, and there are down-payment assistance programs just for you and I, so do not make your inability to save enough money, an excuse to keep you from realizing your buying power.

As more and more millennials successfully complete college or take a break from college, more and more of us settle for signing that lease for an apartment. Imagine positioning ourselves to buy our first home in our 20's, you could potentially have a paid off property (Investment) and no mortgage or rent to pay anyone ever again by the time you are in your 30's. The truth is when you sign on to that lease you are essentially positioning yourself to pay off someone else's mortgage! Someone else's investment. Imagine $800+/month being invested into your own property, each month bringing you closer and closer to owning your piece of generational wealth. That is what we are working toward, that is the heart of this book, to get our generation to utilize our buying power to invest and build wealth for ourselves and the generations to come. It gives me goosebumps to think about bringing a son or daughter into the world, and passing property into their hands. Our children and our children's children will benefit greatly from the decisions we make today. The way the story goes traditionally, we are taught to go to school, work, get married, then buy our first home; for the purpose of starting a family. This model has worked, but has also caused some damage for the next generation. Mothers and fathers deciding to buy late Leaving their debt to their children, from property that still holds a stiff mortgage. What happens when you can't afford to carry your inheritance? It causes more lack than wealth. As millennials we know that we have come to break tradition, and usher in a new wave of generational wealth through real estate. We will discuss more in depth how home equity works and the power of ownership from an investment outlook in a later chapter.

House Rental
Aside from a traditional apartment, renting a home can also be the next best thing and can sometimes be just as easy as finding an apartment. Renting a house is an option most individuals in the twenty-year old age group, never really consider, this option goes write up on top of the shelf with buying a home.

Renting a house shares so many similarities with renting an apartment, and also maintains very distinct differences. You may have to undergo some deep soul searching when it comes to deciding whether or not to rent a house or an apartment. Ask yourself, am I ready to maintain an entire house? For most, the answer to that question is a simple "hecky no", and therefore the apartment option makes for the best choice. Most of us in our twenties are planning on laying a foundation and building from there; not starting a family, but again everyone's story is different, but for the majority, a whole entire house seems like a bit much. When posing the question house or apartment most envision a house to be a single-family detached property, or a house structure which stands alone, but might I suggest a single-family attached house, such as a townhome or condo. Yes, there are many landlords in the business of renting affordable townhomes and condominium units. Not only do these types of properties require little to no maintenance, they are also smaller and typically more affordable to rent. Besides the condominium (condo), a townhouse can rent for just as much or a little less than what some would pay for an apartment. The condo however, would be a little more steep, but hey, we pay for the lifestyle we want. I know for me, my twenties are the years I would love to live right in the middle of all the hustle and bustle. Shopping, Bars, Dining, and more shopping are all at your fingertips when in a high-rise style condo in the city. Granted I must admit that the condo may be a little harder to find as rentals, do to restrictions with homeowners association (HOA) rules and covenants which restrict owners to landlord over their units. At the end of the day if the choice were between a townhome and a condominium, it would be much easier to find a townhome for rent. If the condo still tickles your fancy let's revisit the idea as a home purchase.

The renting of a house works just the same as an apartment, you sign a lease, you give security, and voila you're golden for about 12 months. Local property management companies are your best source for getting setup with a house rental. Freelance landlords are out there and may have appealing opportunities for cheap rent, but it can get messy if your landlord is unorganized and unprofessional. In my day to day engagement in the real estate arena I have seen it all, including tenants forced to vacate due to Landlords who fail to pay the property mortgage or taxes, leading to foreclosure. With a property management company, most of the time the duckies will be in a row.

Even in the rental world, shop around, get the best price, location, and terms that fit your lifestyle and wallet. Trust me your living situation should not be a rushed affair, take your time to browse through and walk through different options before you make your decision. In certain markets, you will find that real estate agents may assist with looking for rental property. More agents assist clients in rental areas or cities where rents are higher, or when agent commissions are protected. Search for an agent in your area that will find the best home rental for you.

Rent- To - Own

Rent-to-Own, or Lease Option Programs are a very convenient and creative way into homeownership. With this option you have the chance to be in the home of your dreams now without having to wait to qualify or come up with the down-payment to close on a mortgage loan. The program is sometimes called a 'lease option', these opportunities allow aspiring homeowners that may not be able to prove current income, have less than favorable credit, or no upfront money for a down-payment, to rent to own.

A Lease option, by definition, is a simple contract between the landlord and tenant, giving the tenant or leasee the sole right to purchase the property during or by the end of the lease period for a fixed purchase price based on the terms of the agreement. In short you may be able to use that 12-month lease time frame to get the necessary credit score and down payment, or down payment assistance, necessary to close on the property at a later date. The even better news is that as you make monthly payments you can negotiate for some or all of your rents to be used as credit towards the purchase price. The option money necessary to take advantage of this type of real estate deal could be anywhere from $1000-$5000. This option money is quite similar to earnest money that one would give for holding a property for a period of time when in the home buying process. The thing to remember about this option money is that it is none refundable, meaning if by the end of your lease you do not decide to execute your right to purchase the property, you forfeit those funds.

Option money does not work like a security deposit, option money is simply consideration for allowing for a lease option agreement. So when contemplating whether or not to do this form of property acquisition make sure to partner with an agent that can help you work out the contract terms. The rent to own option can turn out to be the best option for an individual in their twenties to be able to establish credit, enroll and complete a down payment assistance program, and get used to juggling the expense of homeownership before actually buying. Sadly these types of creative deals are a little difficult to find in a seller's market, simply because there are so many buyers and little inventory. If you are able to find a lease option deal I would recommend jumping right on it, it is simply great preparation for the closing table.

Buying

Yes, renting an apartment may seem to be a lot easier than homeownership, however you will be surprised at the opportunities available for us as young adults especially college graduates. You will be shocked of how much significantly lower monthly mortgage payments are compared to some of the average rents in cities across America. Current interest rates make homeownership a no brainer when it comes to mortgage payments. Currently in 2017, since the market has bounced back and interest rates have settled down, there are now a lot more buyers than there are sellers, or properties to sale. This means that we are currently in a seller's market, driving properties to appreciate in value as the demand for more properties to sale rises. A Buyer's market would look more like a market with a lot of inventory or sellers and not many buyers to buy them up.

I believe the seller's market is a win-win situation. A win for the seller because your property could potentially sale quick and for a lot more equity. A win for the buyer because interest rates are in your favor and you now have the chance to own property at a time where property values are on the rise.

So why buy real estate in your twenties? What is the big deal? I say buy because you CAN! I say buy because you are worth the investment! Once we can understand the importance of investing now for the future, then we can become an unstoppable generation. With your first payment you have just created equity for yourself; in no time your $120,000 loan for example turns into $100,000, meanwhile your property value may begin to inch up to $135,000 overtime for example, now you sell and cash out with $35,000 at closing, and that's just a cute scenario or example. A car as soon as you drive it off the lot, starts to depreciate in value, but property is more likely to appreciate. "Can your apartment do that?" In my Allstate guy voice. That is a big fat no, but the owner of the property is not mad because you are increasing their equity by paying down their mortgage. That is the side of the fence I want to be on, making my money and assets work for me, instead of lying dormant, but we will touch on the real estate investing piece in a later chapter.

The buying process seems like a pretty extensive process, more so than just renting, and I will admit it is, but only if you're going it alone. Which is why I would definitely recommend partnering with an agent/team that will hold your hand through to the closing table. You thought shopping around for an apartment was fun, flaunting your buying power on the real estate market runway of listings is even more exhilarating. Going to showings and open houses for homes in your budget can be extremely fun and fulfilling, it only gets frustrating if you make it or you have a not so good real estate team. Whether you're buying interest is in single family ranch, townhomes, or condominium living, shop for what you want. In hindsight if I knew half of what I know now about homeownership and the whole home buying process, I would have definitely shopped for a nice studio or one bedroom condominium to buy as my first home. Yes I said it! I made a mistake; well, a little baby one. I robbed myself of the chance to shop around for my first home, as mentioned in the introduction, my first home purchase kind of fell into my lap gracefully. I would not for one second take it back, but what I am saying is, don't miss out on the opportunity to shop around, your buying power allows for you to have what you want. The remainder of this book will act as a guide to get you to the closing table and beyond with your twenty year old self!

NOTES...

Chapter II

Zillow & Realtor: Power Couple

Chapter 2
Zillow & Realtor: Power Couple

---------------◆---------------

So now you have decided that homeownership may be the route you need to look into as a personal goal. Once you have made up in your mind that you are serious about buying, then you are officially a buyer, and that makes you powerful! Many of your life's accomplishments and successes start with a decision and a made up mind. So, there is nothing wrong with doing a little window shopping. Look at homes on platforms such as Zillow or Trulia, play with mortgage calculators, and reach out to a local real estate agent. Yes I said it! dive right in. This chapter is to express the importance of utilizing your local real estate professional rather than going this road alone. Even I would not have been able to have a seamless first time home buying experience without the real estate professionals around me to hold my hand.

If you have been renting for a while already you should have a good idea of the monthly budget you can afford based on your income and expenses. That aspect of living never changes, your budget and what you can afford should either remain consistent or compliment your income. Ask yourself how much of a monthly payment is comfortable for me, and how much house can i get for that budget? Once you have that number you can afford to pay, you can easily find and have an idea of how much house you can afford. I cannot begin to express how important it is to define a clear budget for yourself when starting this process. Countless times homebuyers get approved for these massive loan amounts for hundreds of thousands of dollars and make it all the way to the closing table before realizing, wait I can't afford that payment; or worst, closing and now a few months later facing foreclosure. These kinds of home buyers most likely brought that bad habit from financing other things such as a car. They pick out the nicest car, and all the terms seem to be right, but that monthly payment coupled with car insurance, maintenance, all of your other expenses not associated with the car quickly put you in the negative paycheck to paycheck cycle. You must come to a comfortable number, then filter your home search around your budget. Luckily for you there are simple easy to use tools on various websites to calculate the sweet spot price you can afford based on your monthly budget. We will discuss in greater detail in the next chapter, the ins and outs of a mortgage loan.

Zillow

Platforms such as Zillow are great resources and easy to use. I'll admit, and real estate professionals everywhere will agree that the world-wide web has made the home buying process much more streamlined than ever before. From the web you can get pre-qualified with a lender, shop for property, and even e-sign documents, meaning you can potentially put in your own offer on a property, completely cutting out the need for an agent to represent you. Yes, it is all possible however just like WebMD, aka the google doctor, will never replace actually visiting your primary care physician, even so it is highly recommended to consult with a professional when taking on the home buying process, especially for first time homebuyers. Because many aspects of real estate have been interwoven with our modern technology, things are changing every day and trust me real estate professionals stay abreast to the changes.

We simply can't assume that everyone knows what Zillow is, so let's pause and discuss it. There are a plethora of websites that have emerged as go to sites for shopping for homes. Trulia, realtor.com, and Zillow are just a few of the many websites that provide very accurate up to date information in regards to available homes on the market, recently sold, and estimated values. These platforms pull accurate listings and most pertinent information regarding property, from the Multiple Listing Service or MLS. The MLS is an insider platform that brokerage firms use to run accurate comps and prospect homes for clients. For some time the only ones that were able to view information on the MLS, but now one may find almost everything they need regarding a property on these emerging platforms such as Zillow, which seems to be the most widely known and used platform amongst buyers, sellers, and even agents. Also keep in mind that some real estate agents and teams have custom websites with IDX integration, or property search engines that pull properties from the local MLS.

Your Agent

Let's talk about your agent for a moment, and what you need to look for in a great agent. You definitely want to partner with someone backed by or a part of a superb team. By team I mean the agent has a few others in his/her corner that can help facilitate you through to the closing table. Buying a home does not just consist of finding a great property and closing on it within a month. There are quite a few duckies that need to be strategically aligned even before your agent can find you a home. Your agent needs to be able to refer you to preferred lenders, inspectors, insurance agents, and even movers. A great agent with experience knows that the home buying process takes a team to conquer seamlessly. You want to ask your prospective agent, do you have resources in your network to guide me through the process? You may be able to find that answer if you have done your research, their resources just may be on their website. You want to partner with an agent that can at least refer you to a great loan or mortgage officer, especially since getting a mortgage is what makes this whole home buying effort possible.

The quality that distinguishes an average agent from a great agent is the ability to provide a great personable experience. Your agent should be extremely personable, and simply unafraid to level with you on a personable level, to an extent of course. Real estate is a people business at the end of the day people make the decision to buy or sell. With that said find an agent you can relate to, or you simply have a great professional vibe with. You definitely want to be able to refer your agent and/or use your agent for future business. Simply put the agent you decide to partner with should have earned the title 'Your Agent' by the time you make it to the closing table, it should become a lifetime partnership.

You're saying "I hear you Angelo, but an agent that has all the qualities i need has to be a pretty penny." That could not be more further from the truth. It is a common fallacy that it cost to work with a real estate agent, but the truth is it doesn't cost you as the buyer a dime. Buyer's agents make a commission off of the sale of the property at closing, which is more of an incentive for your agent to have those duckies in line that we mentioned earlier. Essentially you could hire an agent to take you all over town looking at homes, but if you don't make an offer on one and make it to closing he/she does not get paid. So that agents do not waste precious time, it is a common practice for agents to require a preapproval letter from your prospective lender, just to gauge your buying ability and seriousness to the cause.

Couple the Two

Why would anyone need an agent if Zillow gives me what i need? Or what you think you need. The fact is, although these platforms are great for finding properties and in my opinion, can be the first place you start when looking for a new home, a real estate professional will get you to the closing table with less of the headache. The help and tools platforms such as Zillow provide are extensive, but have their limitations. Use them along with your agent, chances are the agent you hire will have a profile on Zillow, which makes it that much easier to collaborate on shopping for property. Some agents even have their preferred lenders on the Zillow platform, those are exceptional agents.

Send the properties you have interest in, to your agent so that they can hit the ground running with setting up showing appointments and writing up offers. Once your agent has a clear understanding of what you are looking for, don't be afraid to take a hands-off approach, by allowing you agent to do what they are getting paid to do. Give your agent the opportunity to find a property you will love and deliver on what they promised to you. Trust me, no one likes to work with an over controlling buyer, and i have had my fair share of Buyer-zillas, clients who insist on knowing it all, and controlling every move made in the process. Everyone wins when the home buying process is approached with some intentionality. Knowing

what you are looking for in an agent and in a home makes your experience that much more likely to be a success with less of the stress. Who says buying a home has to be stressful anyway? It really doesn't.

NOTES...

Chapter III
Financing This Thing!

Chapter 3

Financing This Thing!

◆

Up to this point you have been doing your due diligence, window shopping for both the perfect fit in a first home purchase and also for the real estate agent that will best get you through this process and to the closing table. To anyone who is going to be engaged in the real estate market whether for the first time, or twentieth time; whether buying or selling, know that it takes a team to make each transaction a breeze. Agents know this, so most will already have several preferred lenders, buying or selling agents, insurance agents, closing attorneys, and a whole host of partners in their network to help facilitate you. In this chapter we will focus more on the lender member of the team, as they have the wherewithal when it comes to financing property.

All of the moving pieces involved in purchasing property is one reason most individuals shy away from diving right into their first time home buying experience, or put it off; it all seems intimidating and overwhelming. The seemingly impossible process of owning real estate and the thought of going it alone, I admit, would have kept me frozen from making any strides toward homeownership. For those of us in our 20's, the mere thought of homeownership, for most of us, had not even crossed our minds; It's for that reason we should not fear the process of owning, but embrace the possibility. My point is, we are not alone on this journey; as mentioned before real estate at the end of the day is a people business, and as people we naturally are drawn to guide each other. Just think about how eager and ready agents and their teams are to get you to the closing table. As an agent I can say that earned commission is not the only thing we are after. In this business, agents and many of the individuals on the team thrive off of referrals, word of mouth, and your repeat business. So it would be in your real estate professionals' best interest to perform on your behalf in excellence and integrity. This is good news for you because whether you are financially positioned to buy or not, your team of experts are able to evaluate where you stand in the process and set you on the right track to homeownership. Trust me your real estate professionals have people in place ready to help you get your credit where it needs to be, along with a whole host of other preparations you will need before buying your first home.

Your Mortgage Officer

So the big question is how are you going to successfully make a purchase of this magnitude? Turns out the fate of financing your first home lies in the hands of who you hire to help you close on a mortgage loan. Whomever that may be has to possess special qualities such as paying very close attention to detail, thinking outside the box, and has to be savvy with numbers. Do not allow just anyone to handle this important aspect of the home-buying process. Yes your agent may have a preferred mortgage officer in mind but do your due diligence investigating this individual's experience.

Your mortgage officer is commissioned with painting a picture of you to the underwriter as someone who can afford to pay and keep up with the terms and conditions of your loan. This means in order to effectively convince the underwriter that you will be able to amortize a mortgage loan, your loan officer will have to know the ins and outs of all of your finances. Tax returns, credit score, and monthly expenses are just some of the few things these loan officers take into consideration when shopping around for the best lenders, interest rate, and loan terms. Proof of income can be determined by your tax returns or by a few of your recent pay stubs, if you have financed a car before then this process is familiar to you. Most believe in order to qualify to make a home purchase somehow you have to make a lot annually and have an astronomical credit score, this is so far from the truth. The reality is that with the variety of loan types, and state and federal programs for low income households, buying a home turns out to be a lot more doable than one would imagine.

Our credit score as we all know, is determined by the three major credit bureaus, the score gives the underwriter insight on how you manage to pay your creditors. Are you on time? Do you have more credit lines than income? Has anything been sent to collections? You should be familiar with your credit score. At our age, if you're a millennial some of us have yet to establish credit while others have already jacked it all the way up! If you are reading this please realize that your credit score makes you so powerful, especially in the world of real estate, although it is not the only factor that makes the difference, having a good credit score really does put you in position to qualify for a great loan. Please be advised that the loan application inquiry on your credit will more than likely be a hard hit, but don't worry as you start paying your mortgage you'll see that score bounce back in no time. As far as the monthly expenses that you are juggling already at the time of your loan application, the underwriters are looking to pinpoint whether or not a mortgage payment will be able to be tossed in there along with everything else you are juggling. My advice to you before you even begin the loan application, make sure your personal finances and cash flows make since. If you have $2500 in expenses each month and $3000 income, then you are not ready. Trust me you can buy a nice home with that income, you just have to get your expenses under control. You can do that I believe in you!

When I began the process of getting pre-approved, my first attempt was a failure. I remember getting that phone call from the bank and the lady on the other line explaining "due to your income sir we would not be able to approve you". I was so crushed in that moment, but my agent had a loan officer on her team. For some reason he was able to not only approve the loan but also lock-in a fantastic interest rate for me. That goes to show you that what is for you, is for you! Approximately three years after closing I learn that not only did I make enough but had the loan officers asked the right questions, the process could have gone even simpler in my case. Turns out that College graduates that have graduated within the past two years are eligible to use their schooling as proof of income, provided they have at least one paystub of work. That's right all the first loan officer had to do was dig a little deeper, look outside the box, and I could have saved all that stress.

There is a good reason why I used a loan officer over a mortgage representative from a big name bank such as, Wells Fargo, Bank of America, and Chase. Whichever bank you use for everyday transactions, they all most likely have a mortgage loan division for you to utilize at your fingertips but be careful!

Bank Mortgage Reps are more than likely salary based employees meaning, whether you close on a loan or not they collect a check, this could hurt you. mortgage/loan officers are only paid at the closing of the loan, which is good for you because they are more likely to shop for the best lender for your real estate need with the best interest rate, and conditions so great that you will have no choice but to close on the loan. In my opinion and experience, Mortgage officers get the job done. Now I am not advocating to forsake the bank, trust me credit unions have some of the best mortgage rates, simply do your research. Yes many people do still go the traditional bank route with successful outcomes, but it is just one thing to keep in mind.

Remember how I mentioned the real estate transaction from start to finish has become so mainstream and commercialized? Just like platforms such as Zillow and Trulia can be used as an alternative to an agent, you will be shocked to learn that there are also platforms for shopping for the best lender to give you the best interest rate. Good news for you because again, you have the opportunity to essentially cut out another man in the transaction. You may have heard of Quicken Loans, it is exactly what the name suggest; a platform to find a loan rather quickly. That in itself would be a red flag for me, but again I'm sure there have been many successful happy clients. And just like that, we find ourselves considering using the readily available platform over an agent who specializes in what we need. Please heed my advice, let's not be so quick to consider cutting out another member of the team, your lender is absolutely 100% not the individual you want to streamline in this process, especially for your first home purchase.

FHA | VA | Conventional Loans

That special scenario I mentioned before, where a college graduate can use their time in school as proof of income, is allowed under what called an FHA loan. You should know that there are a wide variety of loans and they all have their unique guidelines and terms. The FHA loan which stands for Federal Housing Authority, are insured by the government. The VA loans are of course for any military personnel and are guaranteed by the government. The conventional loan are basically every other type of loan not insured or guaranteed.

For your first home purchase I would recommend that you apply for a fixed FHA loan; fixed meaning the interest rate wont fluctuate but stay the same throughout the term of the loan. FHA loans open up so many doors for so many different special stipulations and allowances, and you definitely want an interest rate that will not fluctuate based on market conditions. With a fixed interest rate you'll never have to worry about your mortgage payments going up due to a change in principal or interest as with an adjustable rate loan.

Some of us may have been a little too young to remember the market crash back in 2008, I know I was personally in the eighth grade, without a care to mow the lawn much less own one. One of the big reasons for the big collapse had to do with how property had been financed. That's right, loans were just too easy to get approved for and the types of loans people were signing were these crazy balloon loans. I would recommend that you stay far away from any mortgage loan with an adjustable rate or balloon payment. Leave those loans to the investors that can get in and get out of the loan pretty quick.

Everyone has a chance at one FHA loan at a time

so claim yours, it will definitely be to your advantage. The guidelines that are set by the FHA and VA are, in my opinion, not too stringent but here are a few important things to remember:

- property must be no more than 4 unit, QuadPlex, single family residential
- The conditions have to meet livable guidelines set by either the FHA or VA. This means you may not be able to purchase a fix & flip, or a property that is less than livable.
- Must acquire mortgage insurance, for the lender's protection against default

There are a lot more important guidelines and need to knows in regards to these loans, however I've given you the most important ones to remember.

Down payment

A hurdle you may have been holding on to in the back of your mind since the beginning of this book might be where you will find your down payment, and yes you have to have "skin in the game". Depending on the loan that you acquire will determine how much your down payment will be, which you would have to bring to closing. If it is an FHA loan chances are you will pay about 3% of the purchase price of the property, versus a conventional loan which is usually a stiff 20% down; the remaining balance becomes the principle that your lender lends. Don't worry some states have programs in place for the opportunity to take advantage of down payment assistance, given you meet certain guidelines. In some states these allowances can get all the way up to a whopping $15000 to go toward the purchase of your property. Look for "first time homebuyer down payment assistance" programs in your state. Of course there are guidelines to follow and criteria to meet to be qualified to receive the funding, but it doesn't hurt to find out if it would be an option for you. Another thing to remember in regards to those programs is the fact that in most if not all cases you will still have to put up some cash, or have that "skin in the game". Most of the time the most you'll have to put up is at least $1000 and chances are you would have done that in the form of earnest money. Earnest money are just funds paid in good faith, that are usually held by the closing attorneys until closing.

Saving up for a down payment can be as easy or hard as you make it. Maybe down payment assistance isn't the route you want to take, then saving up between 5k to 8k should do it.

When I purchased my home I simply didn't know about the first time home buyer allowance in my state. Luckily for you, you have me to inform you of that benefit. I managed to have around 4K ($4,000) saved and my parents matched that to make 8k (my parents rock!). Although my parents made me pay them back each month, I still appreciated the leverage it allowed for me to close. Now, financing your down payment is a little more trickier since your down payment has to be in your bank account, the underwriter also requires an explanation for lump sums that are deposited and withdrawn. In my case my parents match was considered a 'gift'. Ask your loan officer to advise you on how to acquire your down payment so as to not jeopardize your chance of your loan being approved. In my opinion the best chance you have at acquiring a down payment, is saving. I know that's the last thing we all want to do is start a savings, but trust me if you can save about 10k max, you will be well prepared to make the move to home ownership.

NOTES...

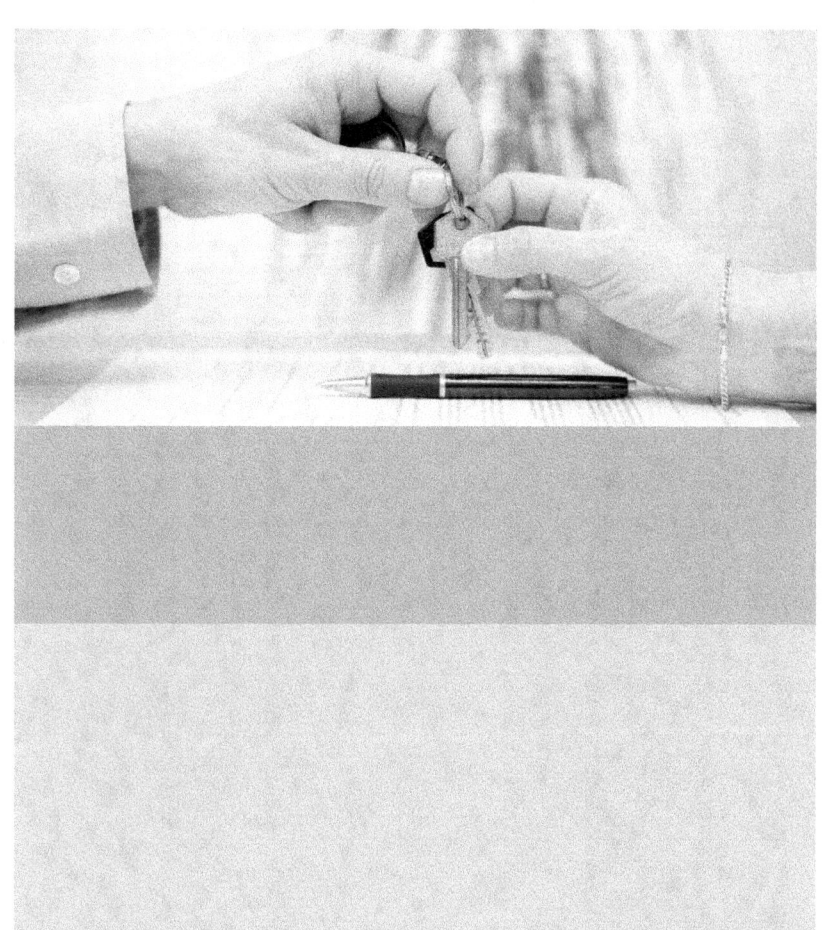

The Closing

Chapter IV

Chapter 4
The Closing

———————◆———————

At last the day has finally come and I just know those feelings of anticipation and excitement will swell up, similar to that child in you on Christmas morning, or the first day of school. I personally felt a combination of nervousness and exhilaration all at the same time; asking myself is this really happening? It can't possibly be this simple, is it? "OMG I get to plan a housewarming!" Trust me you deserve this moment for yourself and for our movement. But how can you be both super excited and uber nervous? What if the seller backs out? Or worst the underwriter finds something that makes this all go up in flames? Everyday there is a closing happening somewhere and these are all real life worries that real life homebuyers are having. I promise you have nothing to worry about and everything to celebrate about, especially since you had a great real estate team backing you up through every step of the process. Your big day should only consist of signing, more signing, and celebration.

Preclose

If you've invested your time into a great agent with an impeccable team, then I have no doubt that the period before your actual closing will be coordinated efficiently. It is during this time where all of the moving pieces are prepared to come together in harmony. From the closing attorney, to earnest money, picking the right Home insurance, and making sure every party to the transaction has every piece of paperwork necessary, this is the time to iron out every kink.

Pre-closing starts from the moment you sign a purchase and sell agreement and handover earnest money, we call this executing the contract in the real estate world. A couple of things begin behind the scenes after a contract is executed. For one the closing attorney opens the file and starts researching title. Of course before any title on property can be transferred to anyone it should be clear of any encumbrances or liens. That is so you, the new owner, are aware of and/or protected from anything negative that may be associated with the property; trust me you want a clear title.

Earnest money, or the funds held as consideration to hold your interest in the property, keep others from raining on your parade. If you have made it to this point, you know how challenging it was to find the perfect home and beat the next guy to the punch. Those funds are held usually by the closing attorney and taken off the purchase price at closing. Earnest money can also be forfeited for violation of the contract and/or backing out of a contract. You want to be sure that this property is the one and that you are ready to sacrifice earnest money for it, typically one thousand dollars. You can rest assure that your agent will keep track of your due diligence period as well as know your contract terms to avoid losing those funds in the case that you did have to terminate your agreement. You simply have nothing to lose, when you are well informed and have partnered with a professional, competent, and experienced real estate team. I can't stress the importance of a skilled team enough, but I'm confident you will have one after reading this book.

There is a window of time that you are able to get your earnest money funds back, and that is during your due diligence period. Most of the time your purchase and sale agreement will layout this period as the time in which you are to have an inspection completed. It is during that time, usually 10-15 days that you may terminate the agreement and get your earnest money back, after that period has ended you forfeit those funds if you try to terminate. As mentioned before, your real estate team should be keeping track of this countdown and moving with haste to get the required inspection and appraisal done. The appraisal will be very important to have completed as that report will determine if you will be able to move forward or not, especially for an FHA or VA loan. Remember FHA loans are insured by the federal government while VA loans are guaranteed by the federal government. Because the federal government is involved in these two programs the requirements and guidelines as it pertains to every aspect of the transaction are examined closer than with a conventional loan transaction; this is especially true for the property itself. The appraiser or individual who will complete your appraisal, will have the final say on whether or not your lender will be able to fund the deal for closing. I would say once this verdict is out, you are home free. Yes there are a variety of other little random issues that may arise however for the most part once you come out of the due diligence period, the closing starts to taste a little more sweeter.

Most likely either your agent or the seller has a preferred closing attorney, in which to transfer title and close on the loan. It is common for new construction communities with agent on site to have their own closing attorneys, some may even offer incentive for using their preferred closing attorney, just like they would also have incentive for using their preferred lender. Since you have a team of real estate professionals guiding you through to the closing table, you should sleep easy every night up until your big day. Anything that needs to be taken care of as far as documentation, inspections, last minute changes, and anything else pertaining to your closing, your team should be following up with. I had an unfortunate experience during the pre-closing phase of my first home purchase. Being twenty years old and never involved in such an intricate purchase as real estate, there are things I needed my team to catch and hold my hand regarding. As my big day approached my mortgage officer realized I had not yet chosen insurance, which is a premium paid through escrow to the insurance company. Now in a rush to get insurance I ended up signing up for a home insurance policy that was astronomical. It was not until after closing and a few months passing by before I realized I could swap out the company my mortgage officer recommend for a much cheaper premium provided by the same insurance company that my auto insurance is under. Make sure you don't make that same mistake, you now have an advantage over others, please be sure to follow up with your team even if no one follows up with you. It is very imperative that you stay in the know at all times regarding your real estate transaction.

Your Closing

Here we are! I hope you brought your lucky pen because you will be signing your life away, figuratively of course. You and your entire Real Estate team; your agent, mortgage officer, inspector, closing attorney, and everyone else involved have worked tirelessly to make this day happen.

In preparation, a few days before the actual closing, the precloser will send over a HUD or settlement statement. This form is just an itemized and detailed layout of where all the funds pertaining to your transaction are going. Once you see the form you'll either regret not paying attention in accounting, or easily be able to identify who is getting what and why. The statement is split up between the buyer's side and seller's side and each side has a debit and credit section. Usually where the Buyer is Debited, the Seller is Credited, and vice versa. It would be wise to review this form and get any questions you may answered either before or have your questions ready when you get to the closing table.

Closing day can be so nerve wrecking, and being in a fancy corporate office with lawyers and administrators everywhere, may even make one feel a little intimidated. Chances are your real estate agent will be there at the closing with you, representing you as their client; trust me that alone will settle your nerves. Chances are since this is your first time, questions will come up, as well as the need for clarity. Don't be afraid to make your concerns known and get the answers and clarity you need. At the end of the day this transaction is one of the greatest transaction you will ever engage in, and we want every T crossed and I dotted.

NOTES...

Chapter V
Homeownership

Chapter 5
Homeownership

———————◆———————

I am so proud of you! You've survived your first home purchase and now you have something to show for your determination. To think you just flipped the script on what's been the status quo. Of course the real estate investors of our time are banking on the millennial to be stuck in the cycle of renting, to pay their bills and make them wealthy, but they can't touch you now! You in fact hold a powerful asset, and as you amortize your loan, you will get closer and closer to owning a stress free, no mortgage, no rent life. A life of wealth you are going to one day pass down, reach back and introduce to the next generation. You still have a mountain to climb though; home ownership can take some time getting used to. In this chapter I'll share with you a few pointers to remember for after the closing, as you step into homeownership and beyond.

Your Mortgage
After making your first payment, I bet you'll be asking yourself why isn't everybody doing this? You'll find that your mortgage payment is a lot less than what you've been paying this whole time for rent. Never to see that rent payment again you now feel secure knowing your mortgage payments are

bringing you that much closer to true financial freedom. Every month that principle and interest takes a hit, you build more and more equity for yourself. Amortization, is what is happening every time you make a mortgage payment; the loan is being amortized; in other words you are eradicating debt.

Of course you remember what your mortgage payment consist of; that principle, interest, tax bill, and homeowners insurance. Let's examine each one for a moment, and allow me to share some tidbits I have learned that most wouldn't share.

When it comes to your homeowners insurance, don't at all hesitate to revisit that annual insurance premium, although you may not need to if you know you've acquired the best, it doesn't hurt to shop around even after you are living in the house. Note that those insurance premiums are a lot like car insurance you should probably shop around for the best rate every once in a while. You will find that you could save a few extra dollars annually, and on your monthly mortgage payments. As I mentioned in the previous chapter, someone dropped the ball for my first home transaction, I simply had no idea that i was supposed to find homeowners insurance before closing. Literally days before my closing, my loan officer found what seemed to be the most expensive annual premium for homeowners insurance. Not knowing how much is too much for those types of premiums

I went with it. It wasn't until a few months into owning that I realized hey! my car insurance company offers a bundle. My home insurance premium was literally cut in half and mortgage payments reduced by about $30 monthly. Again that whole fiasco can be avoided for you with the right guidance, every detail addressed and every T crossed.

Now you'll have to thank me later for this next word of advice. I really want you to lookout for something else in regards to your mortgage, and that is your tax bill. Especially for those of you that sided with going the new construction route like myself. In the case of a new construction purchase, you may receive an overage check for a certain sometimes generous amount from whoever holds your property taxes in escrow, most likely your lender. homeowners receive these checks when the amount set aside for the anticipated tax bill, ends up being more than what the tax bill actually amounted to at the closing of the year. This can occur when property taxes decrease, or in the case of new construction, your first tax bill happens to be just on the land not the property sitting on the land. I received one of these overage checks and completely blew the entire check on who knows what. After the next tax bill came out I received a letter from my lender stating there was a deficiency, and now that same amount that I blew was due. My lender raised my mortgage payments to account for the deficiency, and also gave me the option to pay the deficiency to bring my mortgage payments back down. Personally I went ahead and used a portion of my then tax refund to payoff the tax deficiency and get my payments back down some. After closing, my mortgage payments were about 720, the following year my payments leveled out at around 880 due to the tax bill reflecting my property on the land. No matter what type of property you buy, be on the lookout for your property taxes to fluctuate year to year thus making your mortgage payment fluctuate. Moral of the story, put your overage check, if you get one, into escrow and let it sit there. We don't want to be foreclosed on for not being able to make our mortgage payments. The harsh reality is that this seemingly unexpected deficiency gets good first time home buyers in trouble, but you now can expect it.

Understanding the relationship between the principle and interest from a fundamental level can really motivate you to want to amortize, or pay down your mortgage quicker than 30 years. Your principal balance, is the amount of your loan that is left to pay, your remaining balance. The interest charge comes to slow the process down by adding an amount; which I like to label as a fee for allowing your lender to lend to you. Given the definition of principle and interest, we are only charged interest on the principle balance that remains. In other words paying interest on $120,000 is going to be a lot more than paying interest on \$110,000. Be encouraged to pay a little extra toward the principle each month, especially if your mortgage is a lot less than you were used to paying in rent. The more you pay down your principal the less you'll end up paying in interest. After a couple of years, also consider refinancing your loan. The goal here is to get your interest rate lower, therefore having a reduced payment, giving you more room to pay down the principle. Happy Amortizing!

Your HOA

I am sure we are all familiar with the term HOA, or Homeowners Association. An HOA, is a private association commissioned to manage a specific community. This association may or may not be something you have to consider based on the property you buy. You'll find that properties in a subdivision or condominiums will be subject to the laws and ordinances of their respective HOAs. These associations are responsible for making sure the community maintains a certain appearance and culture, by requiring every member to abide by choice rules and regulations.

Your HOA dues, if any, are due every year to your association and the amount can vary based upon multiple factors. These dues embody the cost to provide amenities and benefits your community may have. Amenities such as a community pool, common area (i.e lodge), fitness space, and the list goes on. If you purchase a property with an HOA, you will at least be paying for the community to keep up the landscape. This is especially true for properties such as town-homes or even single family subdivisions that don't really have amenities but at least require the upkeep of the front sign. Like in the case of my first home, although no amenities yet exist, my HOA collects dues for the upkeep of the sign at least, and trust me they collect their dues every year around tax refund season.

In most cases your HOA dues are taken care of separately from your mortgage or what's held in escrow by your mortgage company. You can inquire to your mortgage company, about if they would be willing to include your HOA dues by withholding the amount each month, however that is up to them and ultimately you will be responsible for it to be paid. Not paying your HOA dues could result in the association fining you or even filing court proceedings. In my experience, my first home was a part of an HOA and they definitely were sure to collect dues every year around refund tax season.

Maintenance
A common misconception is that owning real estate in some way means more maintenance, or headache. Some would go as far as to say that homeownership requires even more maintenance than a rental. A mentorship program that I was a proud member of had us to adopt this biblical

principle: To whom much is given much is expected in return. This holds true even with homeownership, as it is understood by now that owning real estate is a very huge milestone in any individuals life. Homeownership brings about a new mindset, especially when we take into account what it may have taken to acquire the piece of property. A homeowner, whether new or old is just simply going to want to take care of their investment. So if an individual goes into homeownership without the understanding or mindset that this is an investment, than already the notion that homeownership just requires too much maintenance or responsibility will inevitably be present. Your maintenance tolerance of your new home depends on you and your mindset. Let's discuss a few things you may have to lookout for from a maintenance perspective.

We Just touched on the HOA, however you should know that if your property is a part of an association, chances are you will have to maintain the appearance of your property. Your association has rules and covenants as mentioned before that you are expected to abide by. I know I have received my fair share of letters from my association threatening to fine me if I don't cut my grass. So heads up! Hire or take care of your lawn because they are watching. While you take care of the weeds in your yard you may want to also setup an exterminating service for the pest you would rather not have inside your home. These days properties are being built with systems, that only require a quick set up from your local exterminating company to come out and inject the walls from the outside, so as to protect from termites and other pest.

Other things I would recommend be maintained on the outside of your property would be the gutters as well as your HVAC system. If you notice quite a few trees around your property, chances are the leaves will fall inside the gutters and cause damage as it rains and builds up. If left unsolved the buildup could cause damage to your roof, the rain water is supposed to flow off of the roof into the gutters and onto the ground. Your HVAC system, or the system outside responsible for Heating and cooling your home, should definitely be a system you check on every month to make sure it is still operating at its best. You are looking for excessive leaves and normal sounds to come from your system. If you see or hear anything out of the ordinary, you definitely want to call a professional to check it out.

As far as maintenance on the inside the air filter, which is also a part of the HVAC system outside, should be changed every 3-6 months. Of Course air filter sizes vary so be sure to find the one that fits your system. Changing the filter is important to protect from allergies and maintain clean air circulation throughout your home. Another important system to maintain would be your security system, which encompasses the monitoring of burglary, smoke, and hazardous gas. All that should really be done with this system is a simple diagnostic with your service provider and changing batteries on the detectors around the house. You'll notice a chirping sound when the battery is low on any one of the detectors.

Although this chapter seems like a laundry list of duties and responsibilities, you'll find that they can all easily be managed leaving you left to enjoy homeownership and all that it may bring to your life.

NOTES...

Chapter VI

Repeat

Chapter 6

Repeat

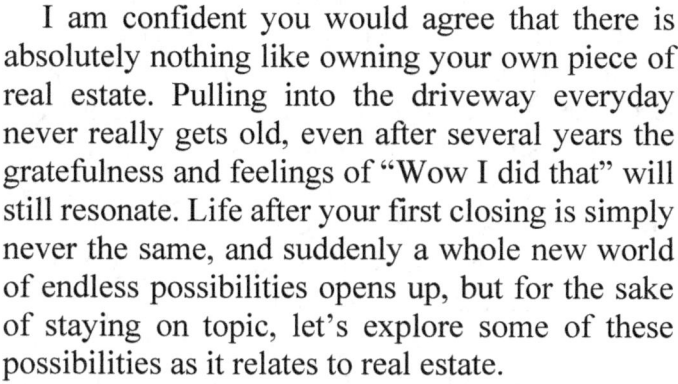

I am confident you would agree that there is absolutely nothing like owning your own piece of real estate. Pulling into the driveway everyday never really gets old, even after several years the gratefulness and feelings of "Wow I did that" will still resonate. Life after your first closing is simply never the same, and suddenly a whole new world of endless possibilities opens up, but for the sake of staying on topic, let's explore some of these possibilities as it relates to real estate.

After you finally close on the first home you'll definitely feel you've got the hang of it, but what's next for you? Once you have made it through the first property, chances are in no time you'll find yourself bit by what I like to refer to as the "real estate enthusiast bug", as I did. In fact I hope this read has shifted some things in you as it relates to your outlook on real estate and real estate investing.

Stepping into homeownership at the time that I did, changed my whole perspective on the possibility of generational wealth. I used to think of leaving wealth to my children and their children only meant getting a good life insurance policy. Those policies are definitely necessary but there's more. Investing is absolutely something we want to take seriously, especially in our youth. Think about how our present investment plans will benefit and position our family after funeral cost, and debt payoffs. If you are in your 20's and already have investment portfolios, a plan for retirement, and or a life insurance policy then kudos. If not, let's take the necessary steps to get educated on and apply investment strategies into our lives.

In my opinion we've got to get ourselves out of the rat race and enjoy abundant life, and I simply chose real estate as the vehicle to drive my wealth to new heights. Can you just imagine your life when you finally hit 30, 40, or 50? living off of income producing property, that appreciates every year, cashing out on rivers of equity when the time is right, and leaving your estate for the next generation to steward over or liquidate. Truth is the "Estate" is what makes the difference, and property turns out to be one of the top go to investments when looking to establish generational wealth. One of the definitions of estate, happens to be the assets and liabilities left by a person upon death. Property is just one of many different types of assets, or investments. I'm glad you kept reading to make it to this point, that means not only are you excited about buying your first property, but you're also considering getting your hands on income producing property, which would be the smartest decision, apart from buying your first property, you could ever make. We have such an advantage as millennials when it comes to purchasing real estate, and that advantage is called "Time". whether it's 1 or 10 properties you plan to have by the time you reach age 50, remember get it in now, and ask yourself what am I waiting on? Think about it, The fact that we could potentially be mortgage free at such a young age to me is a no brainer. No mortgage means less debt, more places to invest your money, and forward progression toward generational wealth. Grab a hold to that notion and keep on reading. If you haven't grasped how powerful it is to have property in your possession, by the end of this chapter you will.

Capital Gains

Property does something very powerful that our financed cars don't do, and that is it appreciates. Appreciate meaning the value increases; As communities progress and cities develop, property values rise. Even market trends can play a role in how much your property can sell for. Something to keep in mind when thinking about selling to collect built up equity in your property, is that uncle Sam wants his piece of the pie too. That's right! More than likely you will have to pay taxes on proceeds from the sale of your property. I want to share with you a strategy my mentor filled me in on; how to take advantage of capital gains.

With the ideal equity that your property accumulates over time, in mind, and knowing that uncle Sam is entitled to his cut. Consider selling your primary residence before your 5th year.

That's right I said it, selling your primary residence before the 5th year of owning it, allows you to take advantage of a little thing called capital gains. Savvy real estate investors everywhere employ this tip to take advantage of the chance to collect equity which is untaxed. Tax laws allow you to have all of your proceeds from the sale of your property, tax free, so long as you lived there for 2 of the 5 years. This is a smart method for reinvesting because after three or four years of paying the mortgage, coupled with the appreciation your property may have acquired, you may be able to attain enough proceeds to reinvest in another property.

The Second Property
When thinking with the mind of an investor, your first home hunt should be for a property you can add a little value to, a property you can foresee appreciating, or becoming more valuable later, based on market trends; and of course you've hired an outstanding agent to help you identify such a property. For the second property you must set your intentions just the same. Set your intentions for the second property, what is it you want to get out of the second purchase? Is it rental income, vacation home, Airbnb, etc.? Make sure you have a clear plan before you get involved in the second purchase; you definitely want to be able to manage

them both. It is true you may only have one FHA loan at a time, but do not let that stop you from acquiring the second property. You can make conventional loans work for you as well, even though the down-payment can be upwards of 20% down, you can save that through taking advantage of capital gains and other forms of aggressive saving, that I would encourage you to employ. I would also encourage you to read up on creative financing in real estate, there are endless possibilities such as "subject-to" property acquisition, that I will simply have to dedicate an entire other book for. Just know that the second property is just as possible and a lot easier than the first.

Landlording
Most individuals thinking about purchasing their second property have intentions to make a rental income. A Landlord is a person, who rents land, a building, or an apartment to a tenant. If you are renting at the moment, your landlord is either an individual or property management company. Even apartment complexes have to have a landlord, or property manager in place to make sure rents are paid, and the property is maintained amongst other things. For you, becoming a landlord can go really well or go really not so well. That is all up to you, and your ability and willingness to stay informed, prepare, and manage like a pro.

Before you acquire the rental property, you should have an idea if you will be taking on the responsibility or hiring a property manager to do it. Either way it is important to set clear intentions and expectations for yourself and anyone else you will have involved in your rental property endeavors. A good property management company is good with screening potential tenants, property maintenance, keeping good records, and anything else directly related to operating your rental property. It may be a good idea to get a feel of managing your first rental property, so that you will know what is expected for when you do hire.

One more strategy for you:
Consider buying a duplex, triplex, or quadplex with your FHA loan.

A multi-unit is a good idea because it allows you to live in and occupy one unit as your place of residence while also giving you a chance to have your mortgage essentially paid by tenants of the other units. Of course the FHA guidelines won't allow you to purchase a property with more than four units but if you can get your hands on and don't mind living in one, go for it!

I'm sure we have all seen a glimpse of the glamorous life of a savvy investor on several different tv shows. We also no better than to believe that investments turn a profit overnight, and although these shows are about a half an hour, investing in real estate or anything takes work, dedication and time. Good thing we have nothing but time as millennials, what a perfect time in our lives to take the next step to become just as savvy as the next investor. Trust me when I say the first property is the most challenging to acquire. With that said, let's move into property number two with confidence and determination.

NOTES...

ABOUT THE AUTHOR

The Author, Angelo been owning it since high school. In 2012, at the age of 16, Angelo graduated high school with a diploma and an associate's degree from Clayton State University. He didn't stop there, Angelo went on to pursue a bachelor's degree in Psychology, and in 2014, at 19 years old, he graduated from college. He found himself in a new and thrilling career soaring above the clouds as a flight attendant right after graduation. Within one year of graduating and starting a career in aviation, he purchased his first home, at the age of 20 years old, and his whole world changed.

Determined to engage with people in a more creative way, Angelo went on to become a licensed Real Estate Agent in the state of Georgia. He is now a top-performing agent with Buy N Sell Inc., serving greater Atlanta and its surrounding areas. Angelo attributes his success as a young graduate and homeowner, to his deep desire to see his generation take the lead into the bright and promising future ahead. His book, Own it In Your 20's, was published in 2018. Although his first published work, Angelo shows no signs of stopping. Readers and real estate wealth enthusiast everywhere can expect more from this dynamic leader.

Angelo Mirville
CEO of Climbing Companion
www.angelomirville.com

with
ANGELO MIRVILLE
Atlanta Real Estate Agent
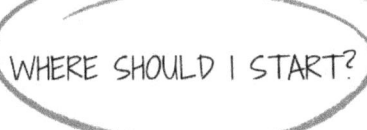

Discover Real Estate in a **NEW** way

WHERE SHOULD I START?

Angelo Mirville Enterprise LLC

www.angelomirville.com

REAL ESTATE CHATS

CLIMBING Companion

BUY.
SELL.
INVEST.

I BUY HOUSES

info@climbingcompanion.com | (678) 374-9007

www.climbingcompanion.com